# MY FIRST
# CHRISTMAS
## High Contrast Baby Book

**THIS BOOK BELONGS TO:**

------------------- -------------------

------------------- -------------------

------------------- -------------------

-------------------

# GUIDELINES

 Do it every day. Show your child for at least a few minutes every day. "Watch as much as you can."

 Let your child focus on the picture for a short time, no longer than seconds at a time.

 Encourage your child to reach for the card and examine it with their hands.

# DING-DING-DING

ENJOY THE GIFT INSIDE
https://bit.ly/******

THE GIFT IN PAGE 25

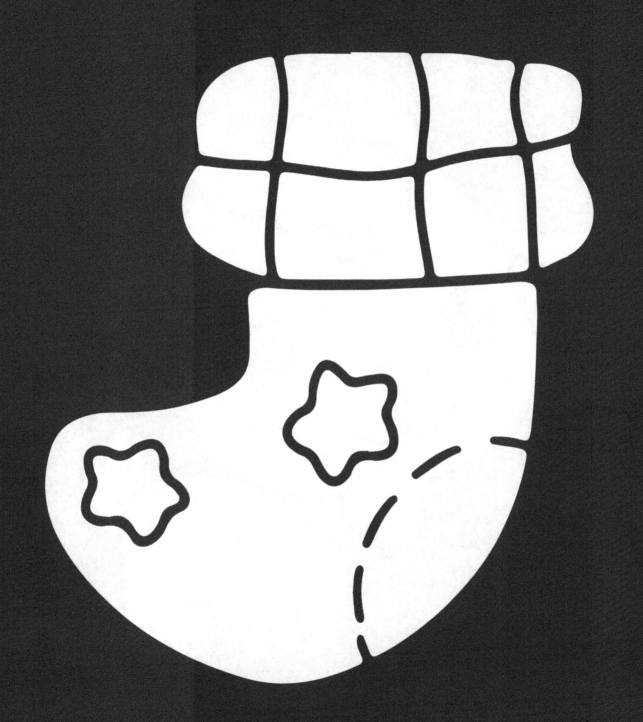

# DING-DING-DING

HERE IS YOUR GIFT:

https://bit.ly/
4f4YOoW

TAP THIS LINK IN THE BROWSER AND ENJOY!
IF YOU LOVED THE BOOK AND THE GIFT GIVE US

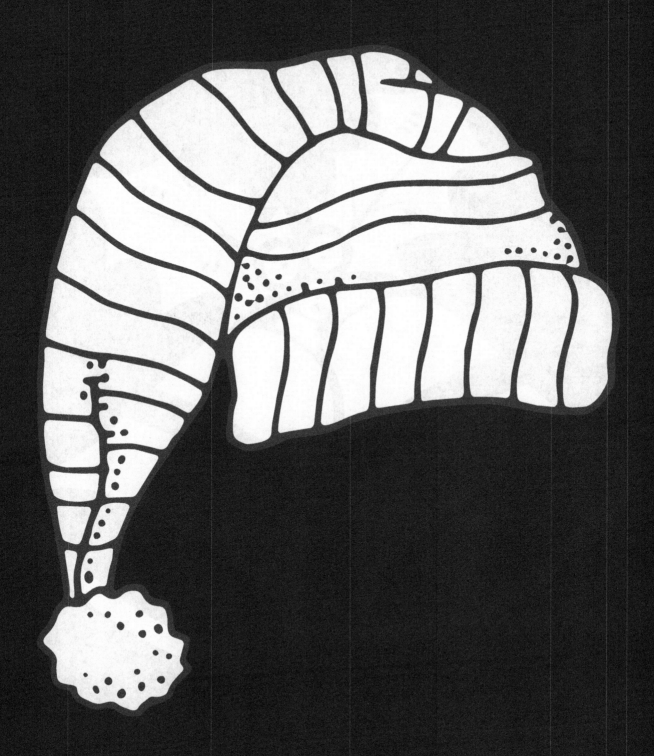

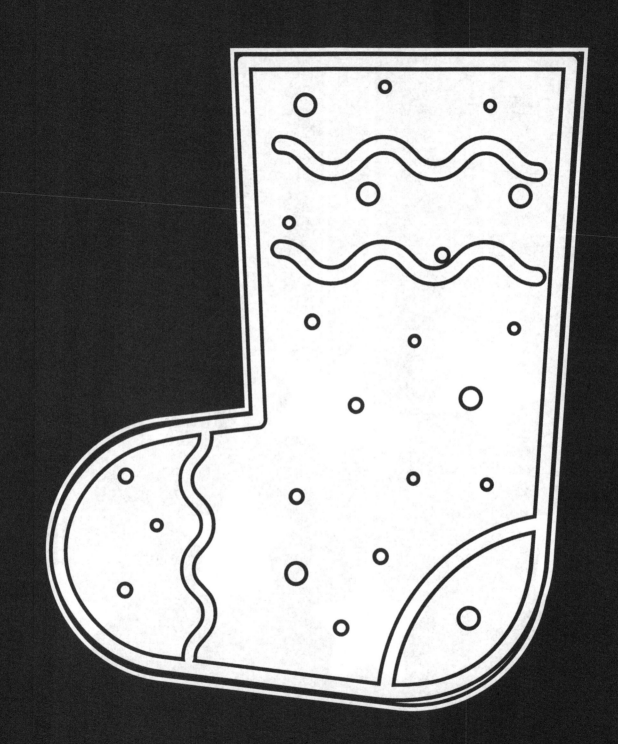

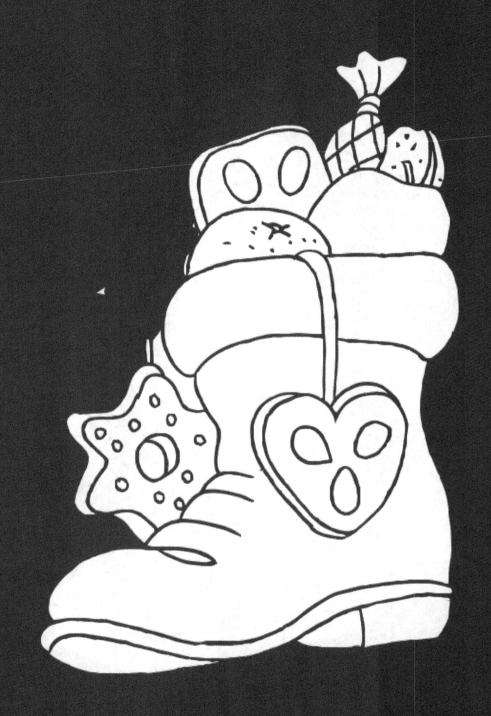